The 52nd State of Amnesia

The 52nd State of Amnesia

poems by

Krisantha Sri Bhaggiyadatta

TSAR
Toronto
1993

The publishers acknowledge generous assistance
from the Ontario Arts Council and the Canada Council.

Copyright © 1993 Krisantha Sri Bhaggiyadatta

All rights reserved. Except for purposes of review, no part of this book may be reproduced in any form without prior permission of the publisher.

TSAR Publications
P.O. Box 6996, Station A
Toronto, Ontario
M5W 1X7 Canada

Canadian Cataloguing in Publication Data

Bhaggiyadatta, Krisantha Sri, 1954-
  The 52nd state of amnesia

Poems.
ISBN 0-920661-37-8

I. Title. II. Title: The fifty-second state of amnesia.

PS8553.H34F54 1993   C811'.54   C93-094970-6
PR9199.3.B43F54 1993

cover: photograph of *Nāga Rāssa* mask, from the private
collection of Suwanda Sugunasiri

Contents

Preface *vii*
Author's note *viii*

The 52nd State
The Discovery of Amnesia 3
johannesburg of the north 5
Friday the 13th. Part 500 7
June 25th, 1876 9
This a little company on a sidestreet in Toronto 10
at the turn of the century 10
1992 11
the end of the line 12
my teacher 13
dear dan 15
I didn't know I was lonely 16
Poems in Flight 17
i saw my tv cry 18
Break it up and give it back 19
Professional No-sayers 20
English as Several Languages 20
we paranoids 21
General Winter Will Take Care of Them 22
Carmana 23
faux pas 28
why don't y'write a poem 28
most english teachers are racists 29
Racists quoting Paolo Freire 30
We could never get work 30
you qualify 31
every morning 32
The Policeman 33
    USA POEMS
Nevada 35
On the "T" in Boston 38

Out of Amnesia
    CHINA POEMS   #1 - #7 43
    INDIA POEMS
Kottayam. December 1990 50
The Deutschmark Devalues (India) 51

Chanagacherry, Kerala. South India. November 27, 1990   52
  SRI LANKA POEMS
  day train to eelam, February 1983   53
  see you standing at the door   55
  less than ten percent   56
  486 years   57
  Amma   58
  1971 from C.o. to T.o.   62
  Refugee Blues   63
  lottery tickets   64
  Lost and Found: A Nursery Rhyme   65
  Forgive Us, Trespassers Will Be Executed . . .   66
  there's no putting things down on paper   67
  you're black like the devil   68
  graduation   68
  A little girl cries for water   69
  The disappeared keep turning up   70
  Mothers' Front Mass Meeting   71
  Who killed ranjan wijeratne   72
  Don't think I didn't see you   73
     VOA: VOICE OF AMNESIA
  Obituary   75
  Rocks for Peace   79
  Let the police do their thing   80
  sit in your one-bedroom   81
  kaunda meets de klerk   82
  A Dry White Season   84
  sri lanka is a colony of anglo-america   85

Read Only Memory
Welcome to the nation!   89
at g.s. woolley   89
so so primitive   89
To The Old White Woman . . .   90
we live in the lower arctic   91
from outside the city   92
all things carry life   92
some people cut the trees   93
Everyday we see you in your newpapers   94
everyday you ask the lobotomic amnesiac's question   95

Preface

In *The 52nd State of Amnesia* there is no navel gazing. No one is running around flaunting ritual flowers or feathers, no one is levitating on the transcendental sound of "Om." Nor is this a hall of mirrors where Narcissus fragments into thousands, or is there enough time for settled agony. These are different, new poems, sometimes anti-poems which hold little truck with "the Poetic." Here the world is always on the move, with a speed equal to the Stock Exchange rising and falling. It is the world of news, of life in the street and in the work place, of the trials and tribulations embroiling ordinary people as they face racism, imperialism and other power-plays and ploys. These poems face us in their staccato starkness, and in all the nuances of the everyday world. The boundaries between prose and poetry are obliterated, joined by a quick wit, a keen eye, and a recognition of pain or despair which is framed with absurdity.

These are political poems and Krisantha Bhaggiyadatta is not squeamish about what he says. He is not afraid to be political. He does not avoid it because current fashion in poetry does not speak of ESL English as a Second Language classes, or the deployment of dictators in plane crashes, or the Octopus-like encroachments of multinationals. Except for occasional voices in black or Puerto Rican poetry, in an engrossing attempt to make the personal into the political, the poetry in and of everyday life has retreated to library margins. Krisantha Bhaggiyadatta however, has performed the wonderful reversal of making the political into the personal. In the spirit of Roque Dalton of El Salvador or Bertolt Brecht of Germany, he has become the town-crier of the latest news, he has invited us to laugh at the oppressor rather than only cry with the victim. He reminds us, as they did, that laughter is a weapon in a war of classes.

In the face of sarcasm and irony, the overarchingness and immutability of tyrants begin to look paltry, their speeches of glory take on the rant of the used-car salesmen. They may have convinced the bourgeoisie and their petty supporters of their strength and worth, but in the eye of this Sri Lankan poet, drawn to Canada by the long chain of imperialism, they remain sadistic gain seekers. In the proverbial wisdom of Mao they are paper tigers. In *The 52nd State of Amnesia*, constructed with memories and strategies of ambush, they will be consigned to oblivion, buried under layers of irony, hidden behind a large laughter of the people, who may not have triumphed right now, but certainly understand the bag of tricks of Old Corruption.

Himani Bannerji

... romanticized into oblivion so carefully observed that many think we are all dead. For every person who came here to find freedom there are bones rattling in our mother...

       Chrystos, *Dream On*

The opening poem in this collection was written for a gathering organized by the Beyond '92 Coalition. Some of these poems have been broadcast on local radio, and published in *The Toronto South Asian Review* and *DIVA*. Most were written between 1987 and 1992. The poem "day train to eelam, February 1983" was written in 1983. Two poems ("Amma" and "Obituary") appeared in a pamphlet, *Mothers and Generals*, 1989. The poems on Sri Lanka and China were written on visits in 1990 and 1991.

Thanx to May Yee and Himani Bannerji ... without whom these poems would've not seen print ...

The 52nd State

The Discovery of Amnesia

1.
this spreading concrete spaceship, toronto:
where streetscape & neighbourhoods switch
like movie sets (on unreal real-estate time).

this age of tele-virtual reality:
(pre-meditated phantasms of absurdity)
where amnesia's bought in one-a-day little blue pills,
(at DRUG WORLD down the street)
and no-escape literature teaching wholesale that:

history began 500 years ago

2.
Apartheid we're taught is something someplace else.
(multiculturalism a code word
for para-statal neo-tribalism)
The latest fashions: Ethnic International,
beauty a mask, for the united colonials (of oblivion).

3.
no life, only work, here on the spaceship.
brought as strangers and competitors, as
troops to the colonial project
now fighting city hall's police
now fighting ottawa's bosses

4.
whenever we fought racism at work, at school,
we always came up against this:
that this wasn't something we discovered
 but had been going on here for a long long time

5.
Between 1987 & 1989: tens of thousands of people in sri lanka in the space of five years were systematically kidnapped and slaughtered by forces trained by the west who trained death squads for south africa, colombia, and sri lanka somewhere in the caribbean

when i tried to explain to people what i'd learned in sri lanka my tongue gagged, 'cos how could people who do not know what is/has been happening here actually understand
what's happening miles a continent and an ocean away

which bring us to 1992:

they say forget history
and i've just started to remember

6.
we learn from each other
from what's happened right here
wherever here happens to be

*when we first came we thought we were lucky to be here, and we were
always told we were lucky to be here. not only that.
they told us, canadians are not racists like the americans
and when we met americans they told us, you know, southerners,
now they are really racist, and both canadians and americans
would tell us: oooh, them south africans—now, they're the real racists.
and then a south african in canada told us: the Bantustans
were modelled on Reservations. Toronto? Welcome to:*

johannesburg of the north

lake iroquois, shore near st. clair avenue or so we're told
drained into ontario down by front street,
left toronto to the traders' board & the chamber of commerce
 (so the story goes where the onkwehonwe—
the first nations of turtle island—
are supposed to have been
a minority even then—
midst majority chunks of ice).

lake iroqouis, re-filled to the top now
with petroleum vapours:
—five years to become canadian, seven to become allergic—
the bank towers from the financial zone flash:
S & M S& M S & M
(S for Scotia's slavedrivers;
M for Montreal's master merchants)
The fur-traders Hudson Bay and Imperialist Bank
stand guard at the gate to the Commercial Zone,
where women are bought,
buy, and are sold.

Here, a piece of the new world,
selling mortgaged real-estate in pickering
melanin gene by gamma ray, a picket fence away
from a nuclear plant:
the whitest neighbour of them all.

Before a car parked outside a house, or so the ad promised;
now the cars lie overnight inside scraper tall buildings,
while we sit outside the house & city hall suggests:
get a permit.

toronto the prime plantation processing immmigrants
manufacturing despair & daily insecurity

the streets run square like plantation rows up and down, north and
south east and west, side to side
half the population works for the colonial office (provincial) which
occupies the blocks between commerce and finance

one day you're social worker next day you're client
(never healing, always the patient)
and it all revolves around panels of wood called
desks. & thinner panels, called paper and a thicker piece called,
the BIG STICK.

(they went to so much trouble to steal it
you think they just gonna hand it over to you?)

Friday the 13th. Part 500

Their movies: mythical memories, embellished lies, dreams
their nightmares, their scenarios, their public plans:

their science fiction movies always have aliens
crashland and make demands
enslave the people with murderously superior
diseases & tricknology
ravage the real-estate, ruin the architecture,
suppress the press
& eat the flesh off people's faces.

(just like they did, fearing it will be done to them now, again:)

their aliens hued or shaded from green to metal-black
always land in washington or topeka, kansas,
(never colombo or even diego garcia,—which is where they've also landed)

their horror movies have a normal family (read: white folks)
middle class, suburban, 2.2 children
all of a sudden attacked by supernatural forces:
normally friendly cutlery impale their recent &
innocently smooth pink-skinned handlers—
knives forks shears and brooms rise to a life of their own
and fly cutting & slashing thru the quiet air of a normal family
consuming car, food, their finger nails and each other

(out of nowhere, just like them)

also making cameo appearances usually are:
the normal ancient and modern tool-kits
of imf-friendly death squads:
the noose, the electric chair, the injection,
the bottle in the vagina, the testicle in the deskdrawer,
the sudden mechanical malfunction of everyday appliances
(with brand names displayed in bold calligraph
or off suggestively to the side):

the exact co-ordinates of fear determined
by the current sales pitch of the insurance industry
or a foreign policy manouevre of the state department

every movie has a chase: a car chase a foot chase
a boat chase; their thrillers: usually a rape chase
the pita-pata pita-pata pita-pata pita-pata
of human (presumed) chasing inhuman (given)
(usually a woman, or black or poor or all of the above)
 pita-pata pita-pata pita-pata pita-pata
the memory of the posse pursuing the renegade indian
pita-pata pita-pata pita-pata pita-pata
the memory of the slaver and his tracking dogs
the vigilante versus the rustler, the imprudent trespasser
pita-pata pita-pata pita-pata pita-pata
the thundering bootbeat of the immigration agent
from the rio grande to these friendly forty-ninth parallels
the world's longest undefended border ('cept against us)
pita-pata pita-pata pita-pata pita-pata
the clicking of the time clock the punch clock
the don't come late again clock
the gasping of the hunted, the haunted, the panic
of a heartbeat: auditory memory: the famed thriller,
the famed western, their scientific fiction:

five hundred years of friday the thirteenth—
year five hundred in the hostage crisis.

(the real criminals rarely make it into the movies
the criminals usually run the companies
that make the films
and don't liked to be photographed)

June 25, 1876

"Your speech is as if a man had knocked me on the head with a stick."

"We all say yes to them—yes yes yes. Whenever we don't agree . . . they give us the same reply: 'You won't get any food! You won't get any food!'" Standing Elk.

1.
The white man is now doing to the world in the 1990s
what they have done to the First Nations in
the last 100, last 500 years

We all say yes to them and when we don't
Cargill, Unilever, Phillip Morris, Booker, Tate & Lyle say, no.
Bush, Major, Mitterrand, Mulroney, Kaifu say

"You won't get any food! You won't get any food!"

2.
Whenever we look at them we think
of those police composites:
yes yes yes these are the criminals
we recognize the eyes, those diamonds, they're ours
we recognize the cheekbones, those hills, they're ours
we recognize the curl in the hair, the trees, they're ours
the street is one long identification line-up of memory
the ghosts have stolen our features & wear it like make-up
don't even take it off at night

This a little company on a sidestreet in Toronto

This a little company on a sidestreet in Toronto
it has a desk and a chair and a telephone
it can sell you a war
a civil war
or a covert war
or simply a war of words

it can sell you the whole shebbang
the guns
the tanks
a mouthful, a cranial sac full
of air
both sides of no debate

at the turn of the century

the world at the turn
of the century:

the boss's newspapers
saying communism is dead.

over and over again.

if so
why the daily obituary?
lest we so easily forget?

1992

the queen saying:
for the first time in seventy years
the world is a safer place
(for whom?).

the pope saying put away your hatred
(against him?)
and calls for peace in Yugoslavia
(what about the dying
in Sri Lanka, Mozambique, Guatemala?)
the archbishop says . . .
ah!

1991. X'mas.
writing the same damned poetry.
the situation's got "sharper," "they" say.

the end of the line

lost in julius caesar's calendar in this western hemisphere
two thousand christian years later
what in fuckin' chris' are we doin here?
a two continents and an ocean away
stuffed, stretched, frozen, laid out
on display — nickeled. dimed. granted.
sucking on sugar-icicles at sub-arctic exhibitions:
snow sculptures midst stolen flesh & land.
blood calibrated, & forecasted
teletyped by the daily dow jones indices.
carved novellas based on rubber-stamped confessions.
on-line transcripts from the torture tanks.
the modern suburban subterranean silencing
of domesticated women.
(domesticated cats
lost and mangled make the front pages)
sun-worshippers.
heresies, and economic heathenisms.
buy and sell commodity dealers.
kleenex-wiped fears.

where this third world war and when.
and who is your neighbour's real-estate agent?

headlines spell the end of history
the end. the very end. the finis. the finale:
"the end of communism"
"post-feminism" and will the ANC opt
for the mixed-slave-market economy?

there've been two hundred wars since " '45"
their multinational news talk of "the war"
and the war to end all wars.

(yes. yes. the end. the very end.
except, of themselves.)

my teacher

my teacher's hard
to follow. one day
she's jewish
the next day she's german
one day she's marx
next day she's with engels
she thinks lenin's
the handsomest hunk
in the world

she's the one who said
you're black
don't forget that
how come you only
go out with white girls?

but my teacher does
what she does
not want me to do.
learn from the errors
of my practice she says
you are what you do
(don't even think of descartes!)

my teacher she's the one
the one who said i had
kings and queens
dancing in my head
(those ones who'd off
my tongue & my head
and shrug)

she's the one who told me
them medieval knights
were no shining chevaliers
but feudal company goon squads
with peasants' necks & the weigh scales
at the points of their swords
bound girls at the edge of their dicks
and the harvest under their boots

my teacher tells me
don't say rude things
about that silly man rushdie
it could have been you

one day she wants to
push the israelis into the sea
and weeps about sabra and shatila
next day she quotes the song of solomon
psalm twenty-two:
my heart melts like wax
between my bowels

black she said marx said
is the colour of oppression

i'm sinhalese, i told her
i'm a lion, you're bengali
you're supposed to be
my cousin. i'm supposed to be an

aryan. she laughed
no, you're dravidian
you're ravana from burning lanka
besides it's all cock and bull
besides i have many relatives
thank you
as for your nation
it's now a plantation
forget about who came first
and who came last
what you gonna do about it?

dear dan

dear dan i've heard you'd gone & died
you the news director : they suppressed
the news and they told me only now
now as the cruise missiles and patriots
tomahawks and the tele-buckets of white paint
crash down on the curly heads
of the Tigris and Euphrates
of Mesopotamia and Arabia
the kissing lips of Africa & Asia
yes

i've always wondered about your thick
black curly hair, the white skin
that did not seem to fit . . . that always broke out
in those dark splotches and sickly-pink pimples
despite all the sex you said you had . . .

now you've gone and died
son of russian parents
who fled the czar,
working class white boy
steel-braceletted red-bandannaed
gay refugee
from Ontario's steel company town

bio-chemical warzone veteran
 fallen, 1991.

I didn't know I was lonely

I didn't know I was lonely 'til I met you
with you I could speak with all of me
I could speak with a whole head
attached to a whole body
— attempt the whole story

I could speak with the front of my head
— the lobe they always scoop —
and with the back
—where they say love can only find refuge—
the haloed crown
which we all have
was ours for the asking
and the telling
—with us
all of us

People tell me, it's maternal.
Perhaps.
I was only looking for leadership
out of this
here
I was lonely
— what can I say?

Poems in Flight

1.
a summer moon full & round embraced us
overwhelmed a toronto night
shed its silver brighter than . . .

a flashlight
fell on us
and flowed towards
our fingers

the tremblings
of the great lakes

in an automobile
started with a screw driver
living off the big three*
by the great five* . . .

2.
i dreamed this dream the other night
and in this dream you
wanted me
and then i knew
it was a dream

and in this dream
i did not know
if it was a dream.
where were you last night?

now awake.
i need you more than ever.

* big three—the auto companies
  great five—the late great lakes

i saw my tv cry

the other day i saw my tv cry, a big gloop of electronic something
form a glassy tear and drip down the sides
at first i couldn't belieeeeeeeve my eyes
i was on the phone at the time, i described my vision
the person on the line said cheap drugs, kris, bad drugs, kris
i just said no, no no no, not i, not i, this is something serious
there's a story in them there seemingly straight lines
being thrown in our faces, like acid etching,
every hour on the hour
 being bombed by them cathode rays,
[an earthy homely version of the sdi]
and then
cryin; that coffin box of wood and glass having to carry
those daily deadly lies
showing the world minute-by-minute valium smiles,
at every instant the good capitalist life
via pop, beer and an always new whiter than white wash,
something's gotta
give. it can't keep going on like that
ofcourse it's gonna cry
all those happy good looking white people
i never see on the street in this world
where do they live? trapped in bank towers?
on the sets of tv commercials?
only imprisoned in mirrors, encased in glossy
4-colour leaflets
sliding snakes through my mail slot?
no, something's gotta give, all that c-bs-nbc-cbc-abc teliteracy
who tell us that the dow jones took a tumble
and businessmen have no confidence in us
"brought to you by . . . " (dupont & ge & itt
and the plantations' owners unilever &
proctor & gamble)
well my television does cry
wouldn't you?

tears without eyes.

Break it up and give it back

Break it up & give it back
Sea to Sea, your chair-squatting ass
More like blood to blood, dust to dust
It's not yours & never will be
Even if you stick a sign outside
& say, trespassers will be prosecuted
all aliens & bus passengers
must stand behind the white line
& register at the door
you're the aliens
you the ones to be prosecuted
you the length of the pressure
on one white line
break it up and give it back
piece by piece
lot by lot
nation by nation
break it up and give it back
what's stolen's not yours
what's not yours aint yours
and we ain't gonna sit in no backyard
and talk it over over tea, coffee or beans
with some second-hand car salesman
who changes the mileage to read
1492, or 1759 or 1876
this is 1992
500 years ain't too short and it ain't too long
and now's as good as any time
 no point going around with your head in your hands

(the only people seeking identities are the cops)

Professional No-sayers

there are college courses in amerika which will teach you
to say no
there are therapy sessions and there are self-help sessions
and they teach you to say no
— not no to the boss, not no to the landlord
not no to the racists and the rapists and
not no to the yes-men, but to say no
to those who didn't get the shares
who didn't get their share, who didn't get . . .

English As Several Languages

there you go again writing to the thief,
writing in the thief's language
writing in blood
writing in his pre-arranged code,
earnestly explaining the accounts
detailing loot, stating place of origin, complaining you, you
didn't get your cut & you were so faithful
to the thief, the language,

hoping the thieved will intercept your
messages
left
lying
on the floor.

we paranoids

we paranoids cannot compete we cannot identify
those following us in the crowd
we don't have the sensors, the heavy-duty
surveillance cameras & hollywood heavies
who only have to blink
open a leaden eye, a shuttered frame
to reveal the hooded tormentor,
standing in the trees
shaded from streetlights and moonlights

we can't look over our shoulders
zoom-in cross-hairs-wise
to rest on the particular
head in the crowd
of the extras. no, we paranoids
have to make it all up
and hope that it eventually fits
the actual story (which is worse
than we can imagine)

so it can all be labelled and filed
under the "I/We told you so..."
category ...
all the strands hidden or discarded
all the staying inside and not going out
all the fear of you know who
all the miscalculations. all the exaggerations
all those infamous sins omitted
all that under-statement ...

General Winter Will Take Care of Them
(Moscow Saying)

General Winter's marched in
no notice of intention, no weather report
the meteorological department was pointing elsewhere,
studying weather patterns in 1867,
there were no headlines. the elections went as planned.
but the voters voted with their feet. those who did vote,
gave much to the candidate with money. and gave less to
the candidate with less. the next capitalist election
will be held at an automated teller machine
you'll use your credit card to enter
your visa will be just that: your VISA.

General Winter arrived earlier.
no warning. just to make sure.
windows and doors are no lines
of defence. glass stiffens and shatters.
wood splinters. a lock is just a token inch
of steel. brought to you by Yale (the lock co.
 not the university)

General Winter commands several battalions
of ice steel cold. the flesh burns and exposes the bone.
General Winter has divisions
six months long. the weak tremble.
the fragile twist. the ill succumb.

General Winter has arrived.
No early warning system. those who gave
much had given more to the Veterans of Foreign Winter Foundation
—they've expected General Winter
all along. General Winter is their god,
their master, their whip-hand man,
their enclosure act.

General Winter's arrived.
enemies and friends scatter for cover.

Carmana

Job Record: 10 years, Major Appliances Ltd.
Geo-political profile: Portuguese from Angola, 1979
Reason for Layoff: Plant Closure. Move to USA, 1989
Present Conditioning: Re-training—English

As if tasting some bitter medicine
a language to swallow
in order to get an office job:
Carmana says,
"i wanna buy *the* ghun
and shwoot that Mulroney!"

every one in the class
bursts out laughing.
"yeah," she says, encouraged,
"i wanna buy *the* ghun
and shwoot that Mulroney!"

we're reading about the economy.
i'm watching Carmana,
the referee at a boxing match
not knowing what to say.
her hand shoots out from her gut
"i wanna buy the ghun
and shwoot that Mulroney"
and her hand in motion is not a fist
nor the direct descendant
of salazar's open palm
—more like a curse
carried curled in her hand
held back by inquisitions
precision pullied by muscles
honed by carrying children and
assembling fridges
"i wanna buy the ghun
and shwoot that Mulroney"

dear TESL co-ordinator
—from whom i have no certificate
and don't really want one—
what do i do?

23

do i ignore her and say
we will now learn the future perfect.
tense.
or do i tell Carmana
she should have used the indefinite article "a"
as in "i wanna buy *a* ghun
and shwoot that Mulroney"
the use of the indefinite article "*a*" gun
describes the wide range of weaponry
made available by the civilisation of chip capitalism &
even: the discounts on ancient armouries
available, under the table

maybe Carmana means she wants to pull
the trigger on the bullet
with Mulroney's name on it
or maybe Carmana knows which weapon
she is talking about
so she was right after all when she said
"i wanna buy the ghun
and shwoot that Mulroney"
she was correct to use the definite article "the"

because "the" gun could mean
the gun the south africans taught
the whites in angola to use
or "the gun" could mean the gun
her neighbour used on the woman,
his lawfully-wedded wife.
the definite article "the" would include the one
one of the people, who used to work
in the wiring unit at Major Appliances Ltd., used
to shoot himself in front of the kids.

"the gun" could also mean the latest
sub-machine gun the local police department
was advertising for the SINGER Corp. in the Toronto Sun
which claims the gun added the finishing touches
to the aerial mass murder of 200,000 people in Iraq

dear TESL co-ordinator
what the fuck should i do when Carmana says
"i wanna buy the ghun

and shwoot that Mulroney"?

should I tell Carmana about the factory that
never shuts or closes down
and produces little mulroneys everyday
so Carmana could go and buy that gun
and shoot Mulroney
but that they have this no-layoff factory
where they'd produce another mulroney
on an hour's notice
even though the name might not even be Mulroney.

dear TESL co-ordinator, you agent of multi-lingual confusion
who actually promotes EHA—English as a Hidden Agenda—
so people will re-learn the new ways
of the old language of slavery
and sing: baa baa black sheep have you any wool
yes sah yes sah three bags full

there are chinese women here
whose garment factories were pulled out
from around and under them
like so many fine layers of silk
the chinese women come early to class in the morning
and practice an ancient dance
an exercise they claim expels demons
a choreography acquired or liberated
from some feudal collaborators
in British Hong Kong

imagine! a dance on the ruins
of the massey ferguson empire
where we now teach english
(the former tractor makers
have changed their monikker
to Varity Corporation) and

there's a huge map of the world
embedded in the wall
with no names of people or places
on which there are only mountains
which stick out like bad stucco
perhaps those are the rugged landscapes

where they couldn't sell those tractors

this map is in a large hall
with ceiling to floor windows
their former tractor showroom
is now an art gallery
and on the walls hang the mindless
chroma-coloured splotches
of the never having to work
children of the factory owners
their canvassed frames twisted and turned
resemble carcasses with blood thrown on them
: like adding insult to injury!
salt to a wound
oil to the fire
the english class offers as similes
for making matters worse
which is what Mulroney is doing

but Mulroney's making matters fine for some people
say one of the class
and another says
yup, there more luxury cars on the road
and yup, there's more homeless on the road
—i asked him where he learned to say, yup!
and he says: from watching cowboy movies
on late-shift television brought to us by mr. eaton

they're all—this class—from Private Auto Parts Ltd.
or was it the Admiral Electric Company?
anyway, one of the class
an ex-policeman from Saigon
who exhibits a profound knowledge
of prepositional phrases, and the fleetingly possessive
says his company HIS company
went from producing weapons on King St
during the second inter-european war
to producing fridges during the third world wars
and now is producing
arms again but this time in Venezuela
for use against peoples in central america
they wanted to "rationalize transportation costs"
his description of the cyclical nature of things

is almost buddhist
and i ask him what are you doing in this class
and he says the CEC told him
to improve his english

what do you want to do i ask him:
nothing he says, i want to do nothing
what do you mean I ask?
he says slowly, i want to be the boss

another says you know back home
you can't say anything against the
government, here you can say all you want
but they don't give a damn

dear TESL co-ordinator?
a teacher told me i should not discuss
details of news-reported plant closures
he says it makes them irritable
dear dear what shall i do
do you think

I should concentrate on the future perfect
and fuck the present

faux pas

oops! committed a faux pas
a faux pas which is english french for fucked up
double barrel english if y'wish:

asked for a bagel in a ukranian restaurant
staffed by polish illegals
who dug frozen donuts from under the dish rags
and said: you wanna eat this?

why don't y'write a poem

g. says why don't y'write a poem
about teaching english, english
as several languages
english as a hidden agenda
english as a civilizing force
teaching english as a way of
keeping employed all those
who learned to say
carefully and earnestly
gimme yr number
 tell me your name
where r u from
and what /how do
you do:

most english teachers are racists

most english teachers are racists
retailers of the embellished history of syphilisation
broken treaties and stolen syntax, computed mumblings
that tumble from the open wound, the mouth
that says one thing, so the mind spells another
so the arms hold up
and dangle helplessly at the sides:

i confess: i teach english to the unemployed
the dis-employed and the under-employed:
that's my job: teaching people english
that may help them find a job

look, i admit, the only job i ever got
was this job; that's toronto:
it all revolves around a desk and paper
one day i'm social worker, next day, i'm client
one day i'm looking for a job: next day i'm asking people why don't they have a job?

Racists quoting Paolo Freire

On May 1, 1991 in a fit
of exuberance
i forgot who i was
& told my employer
what i think
and they encouraged it
and eventually fired me

for following their orders.
Mayday & I forgot.

We could never get work

We could never get work at the poetry
factory over here
and since we didn't have a job
we were not in their league

They said the lines were too slack
We didn't have the knack
we weren't steady on their feet
We didn't have their beat
to bear
which bears
repeat
repeat
repeat

you qualify

it doesn't matter if you, if you
don't know what it is all about,
it's taken for granted
too often

the caller says "you qualify . . . "

qualify for what?

qualify for the survey! , he says
appearing annoyed
in shocked english
as if i don't know these canadian ways.

every week, reader's digest
"the world's biggest magazine"
(quotes are theirs)
sends out letters,
announcing
—to the latest tenant
in their all-brand new-world—

"you won"
on a lead-embroidered envelope

won what?
won the right to qualify
for all retail-capitalist dreams:
house, car, tourist junket

in one deadly subscription
daily.

every morning

every morning rub my eyes
look outside the window
see that someone has died:
a funeral. I live across
from a funeral home.

I wake up
look at my face to see what
i have done, and i look at the mirror
and always in the reflection of
the window, i see the police:
everyday,
it's the funeral home
and it's the only time
guaranteed when you
in a long black limousine
will ever
get a police escort
and maybe the roads will clear:
you're on your way to the cemetary:
little hollywoods everyday
complete with car chase, cops
& black-suited men.

The Policeman

The policeman stands on the corner
edge of the downtown university
directing traffic

white rental trucks line leaf-strewn streets:

they are filming a rock video
a fantasy, again:

a white man is mowing a green lawn—
a typical suburban scene.
red faced with red tights
a blonde haired laughing ballerina
is pulled along by brown leash
worn by a white dog

the white man is mowing the green lawn.
white work gloves handle the red machine.
on the sidewalk the ballerina lurches by.
the dog tugs at the leash
the man mows the lawn.
he doesn't look up or around:
a typical suburban fantasy
 filmed at a downtown
university residence.

the policeman
stands straight up
from the sidewalk
a cardboard cutout
erect at six foot two
at the corner edge of the university
he's just received instructions
from his supervisors
parked behind the house behind the movie. the cop
blue suited blond carries a gun
a billy stick cocked to side
his hands white cuffed
behind his back
he looks up
and down

to his black boots
he looks bored.
he looks at the movie.

a professor white haired
walks by the policeman
the professor wears a grey suit,
one hand holds
a pipe in his mouth
his armpit clutches white files,
striding, his other fist holds tight
two leather briefcases.

he walks past the policeman
at the edge of the university

both nod

and the professor grey-suited is gone
pre-occupied with thoughts
of white paper everywhere,
yellow leaves dance round his shining
pointed black shoes

the policeman turns
and watches the professor

our camera pauses—catches the scene
throws queries to our audience
re-wind and re-play . . .

the professsor hurries by the policeman
the ballerina is pulled by the dog
she walks by the man
mowing his lawn
nobody recognizes each other

but the policeman turns around
perhaps he recognizes the professor.

the audience don't know who is in the movie.

USA POEMS

Nevada

Nevada never does sleep,
las vegas, ever-open ever-circling
fluorescent eye
rolling rolling rolling
black dots on a dice

las vegas's the bomb
dropped on the desert
galaxy of naked neon,
hallucinating, luminating

shimmering chameleon,
gilded gila monster aglitter
(just north of guadalahara)

quivering in a sandstorm of time,
babylon sinking in a volcanic void,

sliding like so many
silver quarters, slushing through
the slots of iron-armed rockerfellers,

born from the death of
hearst's harem in havana
a mormon's memory lapse
(just north of salt lake, utah)
envy of california's crystal cathedrals
a palace to ceasar :
torqouise tower to sexual torture

edge of the navajo, hopi, the d.i.a. and I at
Mirage the name of a hotel, a communion of
coca cola truths placed on
the parched tongues of
.99 cent discount $19.95
total nudity and the nuggets of the $2.95 breakfasts
and the annual convention of the national dealers association

'ey dropped a bomb on nevada
and called it las vegas
a frozen fireworks display
forever burning

success so intent
hope, no not hope
but the possibility
of accidental bliss

las vegas of the quick buck,
the quick marriage the quicker divorce
the roadside wedding chapel
offering marriage licences
slots and live entertainment,
three-in-one
and a weekly SWAP-MEET
for spouses who tire too quickly

what more of a reception would you want?
an american dream built from discarded hollywood scenes
where if you lose your shirt at poker
you could become a stripper in a night club
and if you lose your looks you can become a beautician
and if you shoot your brains out,
you can ask your hairdresser
for the final discount the down for the count discount

a helluva union-made capitalist heaven
a desert oasis under a southern sun
a haltered city of hotel and motels of slot machines,
the slots of the outside chances,
convenience store-displays and dispensable gas stations
maps detailing dead-ends and cul-de-sacs
the great escape literature
of going nowhere and of the best arguments
of remaining where we don't want to be

well-heeled nervous old white men with cracking tans
pale hands rubbing reddened ring-marks off their fingers
high-heeled bored bleached blonde secretaries
walking behind them in crotch-clinging wedding-white skirts
over-dressed women cradling small cash-boxes of play-money
like villagers carrying full buckets of water
on hips of their smooth panty-hosed long legs

over-armed men with nervous heads
dollying large containers of money
undercover cashiers and dealers concealing walkie-talkies

red see-through dice tumble on slabs of green velvet
a woman laughs, a man stands up
the celluloid fantasies of capitalist hope
in one pregnant one very breath-held moment
reel through each player's brain

nat says they change the seat covers
at the slot machines often
because people piss themselves when they win . . .

On the "T" in Boston

they said take the red line
and then take the orange
line
to roxboro

the orange
turned out be
the black

line

all kind of black
going one way
away
from whitey!

"hey bro got a light
don't look like you know
where yer goin'
don't stand by the door
hold it tight
if yer seen
look mean

me
i'm goin straight to bed
cos
they don't pay you on thursday
cos you'll get all shit-faced
and won't get to friday

here gettin' cold
broke
busted
and disgusted"

dover station at 10.30
swear to any god
pray to any god
winter rain pouring through
cracks in wooden roof

is this the third world
or is this america
is this boston or is this . . .

the wooden station sways in
the november atlantic wind

one bulb from one twisted wire
sways through warehouses
dover station looking out over Boston
at the finger wagging dutch finger
of slave trader hancock
of fire and brimstone monuments

the man in the booth
i cud swear there was nobody there
but the man in the booth
an old thin white man
in a uniform
all i could see through
the darkness of the station
and the darkness of the greasy glass booth
was the reflection of the one bulb
catching the rim of his glasses.
A rat flew through my legs.

Out of Amnesia

CHINA POEMS

#1.
a.
taken hostage by a plane
shaken like a coin in a popcan.
i survived 21 hours on a flight.
toronto to beijing. nightless
day following day. two suns at the price of one.

hurtling into a pacific sky.
leaving with some pain. but flying forward.
regret clutching my breast. my empty bags.
nineteen years of toronto.
unresolved objectives. unkept promises.
invisible wars. general anxieties. smokeful talk.

finally shanghai. i ran to the runway.
warm humid air embraces me
like a long lost friend.

b.
Travelling East to West to East
The winds, the agent said, were against us . . .

The networks transmit west to east to west.
The eyes & the brain matter suck & strain
red menace yellow peril black power.
thru fibre optic straws. &CNN warns whites & the green dollars:
Don't Travel to Beijing.

Electronic & nervous DAEWOO. NEC. KENTUCKY FRIED
CHICKEN know better & blink
Behind the trees & the chattering crickets
On tiptoe second floor
they stare at Tiananmen with envy:
Millions stride & stroll
across the square
of the martyrs. of mao.
the museum of the revolution.
the hall of the people . . .

#2.
Conversation:

the hands of the clock have turned
the pendulum has swung from one end
to . . . from the ugly american . . .
to the white goddess of democracy . . .

i have great pain
over the cultural revolution
ten years of my life lost
ten years because my father & mother
were teachers in nanjing
capital of the guomindang
ten years of my life
doing nothing
interfering with farmers

one of those student leaders in beida
he called farmers pigs

but in those ten years of my life
i learned who grew the food
for all who talk of democracy
i learned what most of china
which lives outside the cities
lives like . . .

this i learned
from the cultural revolution:
the farmers are not pigs
the chinese are not pigs

when some of these dollar democrats talk
i remember the sound of the pigs . . .

#3.
The Colonel In Beijing
(On seeing a life size inflatable Colonel Sanders outside a Kentucky Fried Chicken Restaurant)

There you are
and i'd thought i'd left you
behind. old
white man. slavemaster.
smiling your pink-lipped
plastic card smile
on the edge of Tiananmen
the people's square. you
killer of baby-chickens
bring out the old s&m in me.
make me want to twist your goatee
as new lovers and the old folk
pose next to bloatible pallid
polyester inflatable.

the us ambassador drives by
in his tinted window curtained limousine.
but you, dirty old man
look forlorn and unhappy.
red-ribboned chinese girls
pull your ever-reddening ears
little boys piss at your vinyl feet
buried in the concrete
outside the edge of the people's square
where you ain't going.
nowhere.

the us ambassador can go
rage on the range
of his sunbelt plantation
wearing his memento coolee hat
(the diplomatic exchange of the ten-gallon hat
the apache-hunting gringos gave Deng)

but you.
looks like you're stuck here.
the capitalist road only goes
this far:

one block square
of concrete.

freedom of movement
democracy for the colonel
without a colony!

there you are
and i thought i left you
behind.

#4.
a.
the lonely asshole's survival guide.

he travels away and around
from his world. clutching his ever-present
toilet paper . . . he asks the questions
he can't ask at home that
he would not ask of his own

he says he heard
a white guy got deported
(terrible, terrible)
for sleeping with a chinese girl
(well?)
but re-entered under another visa
at another point
a few days later . . .

but everyday in america
a black wo/man is stopped
walking talking sleeping driving
(without or with a white girl /boy)
and is deported to within the borders
of the skin . . . the star-stripped red-circled
reservation ghetto barrio coolie town

b.
a rotating microphone,
his head slowly moves
his face inclines a few inches
his brown hair falls off
one big pink ear

the conversation has turned
to points of interest
his eyes remain on his dictionary
and book. his mind turns to
routes. dates. names. numbers.
certain numbers
1997.

#5.
train thru the heartland.
spear thru the heart.
break apart the skull,
a seed of rice falls

out sprouts purple butterflies
red flames.

why does an urban boy's heart ache
to see the green of the countryside?

#6.
moon. mountainside. rushing river road
just two headlights long
rusty army bus. other passengers. myself. you.
bone. flesh. pillow. board. trying to reach sleep.
round and round. round and round.
moon. mountainside. rushing river.
rusty army bus. other passengers. myself. you.
bone. flesh. pillow. board. trying to reach sleep.
round and round. round and round.
 the same lighted latticed window
diamond in the night.
the same distant red light
on darkened green mountains
i trying not to think.
thinking this is some plot.
just to prove science. just to prove the world
is round. and round and round.
moon. mountainside. rushing river.
rusty army bus. other passengers. myself. you.
bone. flesh. pillow. board. trying to reach sleep.
round and round. round and round.

Kunming-Dali Road, Yunnan Province, 1990

#7.
a.
Beijing's greatest opera:
the choreography
of ten
million
bicyclists

b.
by the lake
dusk air the colour of tea
three generations of women holding hands.
grandmother. mother. daughter.

ahead of them two baby boys. bare.
naked as the world.
stumbling ahead. like two drunken old men.
singing baby songs. songs as wide
as their nakedness. bottoms. brown
and round as the world.
(singing a baby version of the theme
of the asian games). their little penises
 swinging to the beat.

(I must confess I got sick of seeing
 beautiful black-eyed babies
 they seemed to be everywhere)

c.
over Tiananmen square. a red moon.
a postcard memory
all for ourselves.
sent and received. now replied.

besides, where else in the world would you see:
"Long Live The Chinese Revolution.
Long Live The Unity of the World's People."

INDIA POEMS

Kottayam. December 1990

our memories have not painted these walls
eyebrows sweep the railside.
the shadows leave no bruises. yet.
why does every darkening sun
press against the heart

we've learned to look, love, move on
tomorrow another city, tonight another hotel
we may never see each other again
we've learned to hate certain things about ourselves
but it's nothing against what
I've learned to love of you
the wound of our passion healed
our thoughts our needs
made one

don't rush madly against this day
daring the sun, the straight lines
of snow can't capture me. melt away.

— winters don't improve there

— it's not our country.

The Deutschmark Devalues (India)

two of the thinnest brown men carrying bulging suitcases for
this drigible german—lowering herself onto the boat seat
collapsing into stone. impervious. now ignoring
the two brownest thinnest men who
stand respectfully moving imperceptibly. finally
the older one speaks loud. everyone to hear
culi, culi, he demands but she is statue,
albino rock. teutonic ton truck. berlin brick
finally the younger one sticks
his hand out. the german's fingers reach
in her small change bag, putters in her purse
and produces: one ruppee, picked up with two fingers
and then hidden in a fist. extends her arm and
drops it into the cup of his hand. aluminum ruppee
dull against his calloused palm, immobile incredulous
palm that swayed under bulging suitcases,
her eyelids draw down dark metalled curtains
on her reddening cheeks. and disappear into
a book (herman hesse's siddharta)
he looks at his palm.widening. at the ruppee coin shrinking.

infinite quiet.

then suddenly the boat engines start
heads turn away to the roar

the younger man stares at the boatman
stares at the coin. metal
living on the etched pinkness of his hand.
not once looking at her. his hand closes.
drops down abrupt. as if from an old salute.
he turns towards the old man.
"let's go!"

the boatman's body arches, dips the pole into the water
pushes the boat which does not want to move

eddies, circles, ringlets of water enlarge
touch the edge of the land where
the two men stand
watching

Chanagacherry, Kerala. South India.
November 27, 1990

Indian Express headlines the morning:
300 Lankan soldiers killed.
Bush calls for a New Year's Day war.
9.15 a. m. Hotel Vani. Chanagacherry.

the call of the muezzin. the toll of the church bell.
flute on the shortwave. room 608.
overhead fan.

hotel advert claims: bask in the backwaters

a 3 1/2 hour ride thru small canals:
kovils with the tridential oms
mosques with the crescent and the star
churches with the sign of the cross and white jesuses
the shops with their signs announcing discounts

and then the hammers and sickles
on roofless walls, on the concrete columns of bridges
in the deep, dark sparkle of the boat crew

the waters green & blue from sky and sea

woman with steel pot half sunk into the water.
boy cross-legged buddha-like holding a fishing line.

SRI LANKA POEMS

day train to eelam, February 1983
for v.i.s.j.

saw white squares by the sea, white cylinders
blowing orange nitric smoke
at an expressionless
sky

saw the bridge between capital
& country, creaking under the
carriage-weights of plunder,
above the river, they floated
the flowers of the still-born nation
the bodies of the children
(Ajitha said he never ate fish after that)
The Sandhurst-trained Brigadier General had said:
We (who ever that is) learned a lesson in Vietnam!

saw children in spotless clothes
with no books in their hands
stand and stop and turn their heads
as the train flew by on their path
to school, between grease-greyed tracks
and green rice fields

saw a man thrown off a carriage
beaten, Tamil, trembling and bloody.
the train stopped. someone placed his
belongings near his silver watch
beside him
the minute-hand turning crazily
round and round
like his eyes.

saw a different flower every ten seconds
saw the earth turn from copper to orange to red
to brown, saw a mountain black
lift itself towards the sky
like an elephant's head

saw great gangs
of the smallest white butterflies
escorting the train
on either side

saw trees so green they made me cry
saw the land they buried Sinhala children in '71
saw trees so old, shriek and point
saw the pass where they torture Tamil youth
then silence

suddenly it was flat
flat as an outstretched hand
moon-lit long palmyrahs
stuck out and alone
like fingers, like needles
up from salt-white sands

look, he said
old friends rise up from their graves
sit on their tombstones to welcome you.

see you standing at the door

1.
see you standing at the door, between the shops,
between the sellers of laminate
photographs of the Buddha
& airbrushed photographs of Olivia Newton John

2.
standing next to the barber's shop run by the twins
with the uncombed hair

see you standing at the door
between three children all astride you
—the littlest one, cut umbilical protruding, staring defiantly—
your face half hidden by the frame of a plank
your body between this door of panels

3.
i'm told you work in a factory sewing tea bags
(people drop em into white cups in canada,
and then thrown into a garbage bag)
i'm told your mother went to saudi arabia
to keep house for some other people
i'm told the army wants your brother,
and a police sergeant, your little sister
i'm told your father, the tailor, died
a few years after my father died
i'm told your mother built a room above
the room y'all grew up in,
—with remittance money from "west asia"
working as a
domestic/maid/servant/helper
or so the ads said

4.
we look at each other and smile. we grew
up 'cross this dusty road eight feet wide
in two and two different worlds:

"look," the man who owns the corner shop
says, "young sir, why did you go
all the way
to canada
to be poor;
why not stay
(here)
be warm at least . . ."

less than ten percent

less than ten percent of our people
play or watch cricket
yet cricket is called
a national sport
over twenty percent of our people
speak Tamil
yet people are called
a minority

486 years

four hundred and eighty-six years
we did not deport
one white man
white people came to our countries
without the right papers
did not need the right papers
(only toilet paper . . .)

the white man deported us from Sri Lanka
to exile in calcutta, the andamans, malaysia
to islands turned into concentration camps
turning even the ocean indian into a watery penitentiary

exported us to malaysia east and south africa
the americas and europe
to replace old slaves with new slaves
to plant rubber, rice, tea, sugar
to work in plastics factories in Mississauga

for four hundred and eighty-six years
imported Portuguese, Dutch, English men and women
to Sri Lanka
to kill us and to fuck us

we only kill them
when they kill us

we only die
by hands we know very well
by our own hands

if the white man had killed 100,000 of us
in these forty years
of so-called independence
we'd have exported them very quickly

instead they kill us slowly
but quickly
using our own . . .

Amma

My mother always saying you should keep your hands busy
keep the circulation moving, the blood flowing
always make something
for others, of yourself,
always something to do that had to be done
a thousand grains of rice and dhal to be picked and cleaned
of stones and weevils placed carefully by the merchants
for the weigh scales
of needles and threads for socks and shirts to be darned
pants to be ironed
of plants to be watered and chickens and dogs to be fed
for accounts to be kept
to bring up five children and assorted relatives
in a one room house

entertainment meant wasting time
relaxing meaning knitting
all your free time
putting those strands together
sweaters pull overs
patterns and designs from Woman and Home
all the way from England
worn by pink cheeked women and rosy-faced children
and advertised homes with fireplaces blazing
and living rooms filled
with appliances and accessories
and heaven
heaven
meant going to church faithfully wednesday and sunday
a pillar of the church
that's what we said
my mother a pillar
and the church, jerusalem, would fall
without you. that priests would come and go
but for the christian ladies guild
(which became the women's union
after the socialists came to power) that it was the women
who kept that damn church going
that it was you who dressed
your best when you came to church on Sunday
always running after making sure everybody was dressed

58

and me watching you wrap your bluest sari
around your body a fifty times
and put that reddish powder on your brown cheeks
and clutch us and run and standing in the last pews you singing so loud
—falsetto, more like it—and me feeling embarrassed
because people would always turn ohso slightly
but now i know it was the only place
you could let it all out

that you couldn't scream
like the women we would see sometimes
running down the road
who we would call mad and laugh with fear
but we learned to sing and to talk out loud
from that voice of yours
just like you
and who knew that when we sang
how sweet the name of jesus sounds
in a believer's ear
 that it was written by a slavemaster
for the slaves to sing
and here we singing it

and in '83 when you told me I had to go to church
so you could show your come-from-canada son
proudly to the middle class churchgoers
and there i was singing those hymns again
and actually feeling good singing remembering childhood songs,
songs that by now had disappeared into my bones
hymns i now realized: about slaves
and i wanted to destroy the church right then
to pull you out from under it

and amma when i heard you were sick and in hospital
i said i would come
because they say that it's our culture
that we have to look after our mother and our country
that you can never wipe off
the face of your mother
and the feel of our soil
and amma i cry when i remembered how i used to run
down thimbirigasyaya

dreams of you in my head
from the bus and the train station to see you
after three months of that damned lying boarding school
because i missed you so much
and because i loved you when you
you'd put your tired hand
around my waist
and hold me close to your body
and i'd show you my report card
and you'd feed me with your hand
and i'd tell you all the crazy things that had happened
at that place you spent so much money to send me to
where i learned nothing except to be a fascist
manager of a tea estate
when all i wanted to do was read
and that all the books we ever read were hand me down
and severely abridged versions of the truth
but you always bought me any books i wanted
even though books cost an arm and a leg

amma whn i hrd you wr n hospital
i sd i wd come
more out of duty thn wanting to really
and then you said i would cause you more problems
that i fit the description of everyone they were looking for
and i got mad even tho i dint wanna come
cos i'd worried about you
when i said i would never worry about you
cos i know there are mothers across our land
who've never known what we've known

amma, this is our living room
this is where we entertain and this is where we sleep on the ground

amma i was upset that i was worried about you
that today i got up several times during the night
wondering who was keeping me awake
maybe you were dying

as usual there were many things that i told you that
i wanted to tell you
and so many things to ask you that i never asked

i was upset that i cared for you
for i learned not to care for you
for it was too painful and hurt too much
and you probably didn't want to care
because you had so much that had to be done
that you had taken on
that you had to care for so many
and it was a bother that someone actually cared
that it didn't fit into plan, plans, the plan

that it was you whose duty it was to care

1971 from C.o. to T.o.

this is the beginning the painful opening of the wound
first the defenses removed, the old justifications
i'd promised that the first born would be sacrificed
i stepped onto the plane carrying
a copy of portnoy's complaint
i cried on the stewardesses' lap
in amsterdam i met a man who claimed to be a bullfighter
he shot himself with a syringe everyday and gave himself
a couple of electric shocks; he squeezed my hand hard & said
here in the west, you gotta shake a man's hand real hard
and almost broke my fingers . . . england looked like a green
piece of mud somewhere in my dreams today
london encircledlooked like a set of re-done dentures
then toronto
first i remember my sisters, then the highway then
eglinton avenue. one of the first things
i remember don't use metal on the teflon
 & then frying my sister's ladle
and watch the ladle curdle around the egg sun side up
and the first thing i did was turn the tv on
and i watched the tv morning noon and night
and fell in love
with the hostesses demonstrating the prizes
which door do you want?
door#1, door #2, door #3
and then I had to get a job
and then i found out about
door #4

Refugee Blues

kumar works twelve hours every day . . .
he makes his daily pay in three hours
the rest, eight hours, is for his boss. . .
he makes four thousand dollars a month
his boss takes three thousand . . .
mr. mulroney takes three hundred dollars (income tax)
mr. peterson takes three hundred dollars (rent)
mr. weston (loblaws) and mr. eaton take two hundred dollars
(food etc.)
he sends two hundred home . . .
shanthi worked for three years in a restaurant in germany
she made three thousand marks, gave it to sella
as advance payment
on a dowry, who blew it on some brown . . .

yeah. this is my plan:
sister's dowry. parents from Jaffna
to India. a vcr. a car
a house in suburbia.

lottery tickets

my grandmother bought those gymkana tickets every week
and my mother bought them lottery tickets every thursday after
payday

in scarboro the other day my niece
was busy scratching the numbers
on the weekly wintario

and today here i am
waiting for my numbers to come up!

altogether four
generations we span
one hundred years
buying everyday a little wish
buying retail
a little piece of bourgeois fantasy

that prince/ss charmin' may come along
that you might hit it lucky
that despite all the other slaves just like you
—scratching, rubbing,
tearing down the dotted line—
opening the envelope, please!
you are going to win

one hundred years!
enough!
let's rob a bank!

Lost And Found: A Nursery Rhyme*

two young girls who never came home again
two young girls who went to school one day
two young girls who didn't make it beyond them gates
two young girls who were videotaped (at the student strikes)

TWO GIRLS FOUND DEAD:
there were no headlines like that.
& they were not found

except on police videotapes . . .

the authority said "mother
were your children political?"

no. they were my two young girls . . .

"well then, let's look at the videotapes . . .
 aahh! they're they are . . . isn't that them
in the school yard?
raising their arms raising their fists
kicking up the dust!
now what d'yu have to say . . .
what d'yu have to say???"

* from an interview with a news editor

Forgive Us, Trespassers Will Be Executed...*

three young boys told to kneel:
worship that bank of ceylon, they
were recovering for their new economy
(robbing, said the News)
for their revolution.

then, three bullets
into three young heads
multiplied by 2,000
people old and other
day work done
standing at the crossroads
busstop, watching . . .
even the lottery seller
stops his crying . . .

(eight weeks later
 the president announces
that $6 billion ruppees
in BOC loans to "big" people,
have been forgiven)

* from an interview with a news editor

there's no putting things down on paper

"there's no putting things down on paper
look at that gay boy, they even took his diaries
before they shot him. me, it's all there in my head
and i drown it every day in booze
it's my native right, my friend
it's my native right
don't come here with your english poetry
and your western ideas . . ."

you're black like the devil

you're black like the devil.
me, yes i'm black, but my soul is white
yes it is.

and what you speak. is of the devil
and out of your mouth comes devilish things . . .

jesus a black man . . . what rubbish!
he was white and pure . . .

(reaction from my aunt that the
painting of jesus they've been worshipping
all these years,
could be a gay italian model from milano.)

graduation

there have been two great graduation
ceremonies since paper independence

1971.
1989.

can't wait for the next exam.

(Compare scores with 1505, 1658, 1795, 1815, 1848)

A little girl cries for water

A little girl cries for water.
he gets down from the stage, his speech.
lifts the child to arms
pours water into her mouth.
the crowd goes wild. people dancing.
kicking up dust. touching the ground
he walks on.

He tells the village:
this polios you fed me
is better than all the meat and fish
I eat in Colombo . . .

In every village, when the gentry
bring him food—he picks it up
goes sit with the beggars
and eats with his hand . . .

He's marched thru Colombo
wearing a tattered sarong . . .

there's no one to
out-populist the president,

sudha says:

buddhism in his mouth.
mass murder in his gut.

The disappeared keep turning up

The disappeared keep turning up
on perfectly happy days
In polite conversations that ask about
so and so
In arguments where the very existence
of the disappeared is disputed
On walls where the graffiti
is overgrown with lichen and movie posters
In passing glimpses
of the hair of upturned brooms
In looking in the mirror alone
and finding no one there
or finding several faces you once knew
The disappeared keep turning up
even in the emptied newspaper columns
 In the lighted rooms bereft of shadows
And then you find out that the disappeared
exist within large boundaries of land
which you have never visited
in documents which you have never read
under several shovelfuls of earth
and several annual baptisms of snow

they exist in your very backyard in the chair
you are sitting next to
the food you eat
passed under their noses
and then you find out
their existence was only disappeared
from your two small eyes
the numbers adddresses and
dates never made
it into your single books
into your one bedroom
so many walls blanked
in your one small mind

Mothers' Front Mass Meeting

Mothers' Front Mass Meeting. February 19, 1991
Defense Minister Blown Up. March 2, 1991

it seemed so sudden
—that aura of hate—
suddenly, gone:
A cloud of smoke!

(the priest quoting someone:
life, but a vapour).

All his victims died
slow tortuous

60,000 deaths
says the economist
so economically

but he died quick!
Maybe it was the Minister of Justice!

Who killed ranjan wijeratne

Who killed ranjan wijeratne
it must have been god
because god is so compassionate
particularly, to the rich
in a country where women and men
die slower and at greater rates
ranjan wijeratne died at an instant
flash of remote-controlled supernova along with his most-feared
head, rear and bodyguards
the sas-trained stf . . .
and the usually unnamed innocent by-standers

was it? the unp or the ltte or the jvp
was it the cia or mi5 or raw or mossad.
or was it a singapore casino owner or
the corporation unilever?
it don't matter; a junior defence minister
(made a posthumous general
by a humourous president
at a mafia funeral
where assassins offer up
condolences to other assassins)

ranjan gone to parliamentary heaven
attained nibbana and is now re-born
as a poor villager with no udawa
and no relations among
the kotelawalas, the senanayakes or the jayawardenes
the ratwattes, the wijewardenes or the obeysekeras
on the run from the prra the green tigers
the black cats all those
off-duty security-men
earning double-time and a half
doing piece-work paid per extracted finger-nail
severed eye, burst eardrum, testicle
seared vagina & rectum

Don't think I didn't see you

Don't think I didn't see you. Don't think I didn't
know you were there.
Don't think I looked away, because I did indeed look away
Don't think I didn't see your eyes so black and so red
Don't think I didn't want to talk.
To ask you so many questions
I just didn't know what to say. I didn't know where to start . . .
Every word was swallowed way down in my throat
So I tried to eat quickly —such good food, i said—
Everything seemed like I tried not to see you
Seemed like I tried not to know you were there
Tried not to look into your red eyes
and looked instead at your son's, don't they look those eyes
like his father's I said, and I
Saw you look so tired, and so tough,
and look at me kinda like I was wasting your time
Kinda like: not only do we die,
we have to answer questions from the killers
and help construct their alibis and conscience;
so I didn't want to say anything, everything
I thought of seemed so foolish
everything i tried to say couldn't be said
what else is there to say.—my, the food is so nice!—
what else is there to ask. everyone knows what happened
everyone just has that look in their eyes
all the children looking seven going on seventy
I couldn't talk to them, and tried to talk kidstalk
but they just looked at me and it was I
who felt like a child, felt I'd lived on borrowed time
time taken from them, an old man acting like a child
grow up grow up they seemed to cry

nandana says there were bodies burning at the corner
and dayanthi the younger one says, ooooh everywhere everywhere
near my school there were so many, says Maithri
and little harsha says killed them and threw them away

and they are all under ten . . .

*before they're ten in america the children see
ten thousand murders
on television, all those no death deaths
and now that bush murdered a hundred thousand in a month
and a hundred thousand more children are expected to die
the magician swings his golf arm,
and the death box switches channels*

VOA: VOICE OF AMNESIA

Obituary

well, august's normally winding down time,
the month before the leaves turn
winter holding its breath
the ruling class on vacation, again

it's been a great week, a great Wednesday
wasn't it? the fascist diktator Zia Al Haq died
a tyrant is dead, or should we say tyrants are dead
it isn't every day when seventeen generals
fall from the sky (without a parachute)
We normally don't celebrate death.
But they were mass-murderers, not the kind of sensational
mini-mass murderers, you regularly see on teevee or
on the front pages of the Star, the Globe & the Sun
like Clifford Olson, Jim Jones or some other
with a stubble or a beard and thick glasses
who the papers say was unemployed or insane
and killed ten people,

these mass-murderers are the ruling kind
who sell wholesale and murder wholesale
and live retail and eat and drink
in a day what people eat in a year

these were not the mass-murderers or terrorists
of the National Enquirer's non-inquiries
of the Toronto Starry-eyes, or the Hamilton Spectator's Sports
These were mass-murderers
who were elegantly dressed in suits and uniforms
who were handsome grotesques with their groomed short hairs
who had shining medals tinkling like coins up and down
their inflatable chests!
who live off the minimized wages of their people
who chase their people as immigrants & refugees
to slave on foreign shores!
who use their armies to kill their own people
who trade away their people's sovereignty
who sell the labour of children not yet born

for military grants, defense contracts,
swiss bank accounts, hamburger franchises &
corner shops around the world
who give over their land to foreign mercenaries
to wage war on neighbouring countries

we see the Globe & Mail wrote Zia an obituary
we see the tee vee news avoided mention of
the US ambassador and the US generals
who were also on that plane
These Useless generals who are oriental spiritualists
& specialists on genocide
(veteran descendants of Wounded Knee)
who lead the rapid deployment forces
stationing 50,000 marines on Diego Garcia in the Indian Ocean
so that they may attack anywhere in Asia or Africa
where most people of the world also live
hence where the great wealth of the world also lies
those US generals who see the Indian Ocean as a swimming pool
or lily pond of multinationals
just like they see and once saw the Caribbean
through the ice of grounded glass

well, we see the freely-trading Prime Minister Brian Mulroney
has sent his regrets about the dictator General Zia & friends

we wonder what Mulroney regrets
does he regret he could not do what the fascist Zia did?
does he regret Mulroney could not do
what white people have already done in the Americas
is he jealous? does Mulroney regret
he could not murder (like Zia did when he was but a colonel)
thousands of Palestinians in Jordan in September, 1970
does Mulroney regret he hasn't hundreds of political prisoners
in the jails like Zia did?

we can't remember if the Canadian government
sent regrets when Hitler died, or Mussolini
the people of the world don't regret
the people of the world regret
the people of the world won't forget
despite Mulroney's regrets

despite Mulroney's regrets,
Zia was a mass-murderer
who has sent 20,000 soldiers to guard
the false kings of Saudi Arabia & Middle East
to make sure that easy oil was siphoned
into the tankers of multinational corporations
this Zia who's been promised $4.2 billion dollars
in US military money
this Zia who helped introduce the oh-so-ordinary
and the nuclear weaponry
of mass-destruction into the Indian Ocean
this Zia who trained junior officers in Sri Lanka
and passed off second-hand used-weapons
(while Britain and Israel trained death-squads
of elite tea drinkers)
who murdered Baluchis in the mountains of Baluchistan
who sent pilots to fly Iraqi jets with chemical bombs over Iran
this is the man Mulroney regrets
this Zia who declared, a woman is half a man
this Zia who called himself the shadow of Allah
but was really the shadow of death

Mulroney's regrets fall like
so many beads of
oil in an ocean of blood

Z-I-A or C-I-A
it don't matter how you spell
his name. Zia so long
Zia, see ya later, buddy
we only wish things were so easy

my only regret is that
we may not have mentioned everything
the fascist Zia and his kronies did
history, please excuse us

*well, I can't remember feeling so good since '79
and no one else reminds us of that great year
better than the Trinidadian calypsonian The Mighty Sparrow
who sang of all those dictators who fled
to become "Wanted Men":
"the rule of the tyrants decline, the year 1979."*

**dedicated to the General Zias, General Somozas, General Parks
General Motors, General Foods, Bothas, Gaireys, Salazars all those other
fascists in General**

PS
*when I look back at the poem, it sounds vengeful
perhaps, reactionary
but sad to say I enjoyed reading it in '88
but later that week, the Financial Times of London
which said the capitalists were unhappy with Zia
because the rate of profit had fallen . . . besides
the man who took over is Pakistan's oldest CIA agent*

anyway another poem, once and f'all:

Zia Al Haq who said
a woman is half
a man

today is not even
a leg or a hand . . .

Rocks for Peace*

lift up our eyes up to the hills
beyond colonel macleans' headlines
see the helicopter gunships of the free press
see roads of refugees fleeing the cross-hairs of their lenses
see most modern missiles falling in the valley of bekaa
see immigration officers asking the tough questions
they never ask their ancestors
see missions of peace sponsored by nobel arms merchants
see the international monetary fund issuing deadlines
see a train disappearing loaded with the harvests

raise our eyes up to the hills
from whence the holy stones roll
forget water into wine
turn them slingshots into AK-47s . . .

*On Palestinian T-shirt seen in Beijing

Let the police do their thing

News Item: On Thursday, before Trade Union leader Rolando Olalia's death was confirmed, Filipino Defence Minister Juan Ponce Enrile said he knew nothing about the opposition leader's disappearance. He told reporters yesterday: "Let the Police do their thing."

Poetic Item:
Let the police do their thing
Like the army did (for Benigno)
Like the judges do, let them
do their thing, like the airbase & naval thing
Like the (Dole plantation-owners') guard dogs
Let them do the Benigno thing
Lets all clap and sing
(Let them do the Malcolm X
and the Martin Luther King)
Let the factory owners' children
do their left-wingy thing
Let them do the microscope
and the stethoscope
and the telescope
(let's get some distance on this thing)
the "missing persons" form thing
Let them do the Watergate
and the Unexpurgated thing
Let them do an inquest
a review, a post-mortem
a royal commission
a report, a series of memos
Let them tell you
"it's in the mail"
"it's at the final stage"
"its being returned to you for
 further information"
or assure you
if you didn't know
"it's in the system"
let's all disappear

sit in your one-bedroom

sit in your one-bedroom
look out the window
watch the rain come down
if you don't get wet
can't say it's raining
maybe out there maybe ten
minutes away
there's a war on
someone's screaming
a wall away
someone's falling down
but it's not wet over here
here in the one-bedroom
here by the television
there's lightning
there's thunder
there's the fire engines
and the ambulance
every few minutes
on cue
it's not you
yet
here it's dry and warm
here there's food in the mouth
here there is no accident
yet.

kaunda meets de klerk

today the black & white photographs
on all the front papers
of newspages all over
written on the faces
of the white world,

a black man's seen shaking hands
with these white men
watching the camera for the camera
saying S M I L E
saying zambia is safe
for now for them

in his left hand
mr kaunda carries a white handkerchief
de klerk is ringed wit de special white police

(everything's a secret there
& the police are special)

on a black table
a white page
flutters at the tip
of a black pen, a black finger

the usual black & white
security men . . .

next day, another photograph: a black woman's head
between several white heads of women
on a bus

these photographs wear a necklace of words
words that shake hands and smile
words that assure the readers,
the half a million fifty-cent investors
of mr thomson's globe and mail,
his simpson department store employees,
his thomson hotel and travel operators
on white beaches, hotels and in buses everywhere
that business's as usual

that the shining cash registers ring and
the black cashiers sing: christmas
is happening everyday

happy together
the black woman and these white women
travelling down on this white bus
on this same black road
stopping at a different address
stopping at the same address
—different entrances, different exits—

joy in the worlds of bay street
as it is in market street
in pretoria as it is in ottawa

some to the world of gold bracelets
the rest to the iron handcuffs
to the streets that necklace the words
that necklace the photographs
of faces of the white world

one day a tire wheel flies off
one day a necklace burns . . .

A Dry White Season

mr marlon brando tells mr thomson's globe and mail
that much of the celluloid much
of the truths of Southern Africa today
fell down down
 on the cutting room floor
as do many suspects onto the sidewalks
of john vorster square

the globe and mail's fashioned film critics provide us
with the thoughts of and about mr. brando
his septuagenarian sexiness
his gratitude for thomson's national
newspaper's set of questions
on the natives and the national question

mr brando has made many movies
why is this a surprise?
can't he negotiate a comprehensive contract
can't a million dollar honky obtain
what a million mine workers cannot?

will millions of our five dollar film tickets
go to the anc pac bcm udf azapo

or will they make more moving photographs
of us tickets /ballots, in hand
that take us nowhere?

sri lanka is a colony of anglo-america

1.
sri lanka is a colony of anglo-america (unilever)
kenya is a colony of anglo-america (lonrho)
southern africa is a colony of anglo-america (anglo-american) the americas are a colony of anglo-america (period.)

when sa is liberated the lords of the english will
have to work like everybody else
england will become a developing country . . .
kenya will be, sri lanka will be
america will be
(then we'll see who won the second european tribal war)

2.
seran says we're not the third world
we're number one

that's right!
we's the world!
them's the minority!

now what?

3.
intelligence report # 365

dateline: everyday
right before our eyes
in the golden heat of the day
in the silk pitch of the night

black men meet
in the deep-us
the most danger-us
mines in the world

darkest africa indeed!

4.
rock and roll telephone:

yez baby . . . it's you and me
   . . . and the rcmp

listening devices need wires
bell telephone and mother AT & T need copper
Chile gets pinochet

itt spent
six million dollars
to murder a hundred thousand
women and men
in three weeks.

click.
the phone goes dead.
hello. hello. is anybody there?
the andes bleeds
our mouths bleed
electrode of a telephone

confess now or later.
go on. make that call.

Read Only Memory

Welcome to the nation!

Your home on native land!
Toronto the plantation!
Take a number
And take your stand!

Why did you come to Toronto?
For the scenery and the architecture?
For the swampy air?

at g.s. woolley

at g.s. woolley
in scarborough
every night
women of korea greece hong kong
mold the sparkling chrome
for cosmetic nameplates
papersmooth the rubber balls
of stickshifts over which
highly painted white
 young women and men
will rub their hands
on television commercials
to sell the dreams
that go nowhere
in the fast lane, ofcourse . . .

so so primitive

so the amer indians and the africans and the rest
of us, the world—so so primitive.
starvation, homelessness and mandatory cold . . . so so modern.

To The Old White Woman
Being Taken Out On A Stretcher
At The Old Age Home—Christie Pits

So what did you gain
after 500 years?
what did you discover?
Seeing you carried
out in agony,
your orange-pink
lipstuck lips
shaped in the O of pain
your purple rimmed eyes
your face to the side
away from your final home
(mortgage payments paid)
on a white stretcher
covered in white sheets
being hustled into a white van
by smirking white men
being shipped from this
modern warehouse of death
wires here wires there
wires in your arms
wires in your nose
straps around your hands

where your daughter
where your son
what did they tell you
when you got married
where that man
and where those endless hours
watching that coffin,
that box
of bubbles . . . , the foam
those lips . . .

we live in the lower arctic

we live in the lower arctic
in maximum toronto, down from upscale despair

here it is police budget month;
the public's blood flows freely
on the front pages
the newspapers promise and threaten

saturday morning: five young black men with sticks upraised
(all the way from soweto)
greet the lounging weekend reader
of the globe and mail

the papers are full of heads being broken
for no apparent reasons;
women being murdered for
all the apparent reasons; sensational
trials being heard in court
pockets are being picked, houselocks too
prisoners on the verge of escaping banks being robbed
mass-murderers prowling malls
the police look after mr. eaton
mr. eaton looks after the police

the numbers appear, appear and disappear
the dow jones index, the gold, the silver
and the daily body count.

from outside the city

from outside the city, it's apparent
the cities are burning
but we living in't; don't know it
our minds turn to
the knock on the door; the letter
through the slot;
the ring of the telephone;
the screaming of tires
the reaching for the cigarette
the dance of the shifting
round the flickers of the lighted tube

all things carry life

all things carry life
and many stories can be heard
but the silence of things is all you've heard about
and stones tell no tales

but look
the walls of the city
you built to hide
are crumbling
the promised castle in desert sands

some people cut the trees

some people cut the trees, some people pulp it
some people shape the wood
into batons that pulp people's brains
some people stick the limbs and arms together
so that social workers and teachers can sit in these chairs
and slide paper around like it was money:
sign this, and is this the truth
the whole truth and nothing but
answer all of the above

Everyday we see you in your newspapers

Everyday we see you in your newspapers
holding up your daily headlines
against me
(these are your picket signs)

Everyday we see you screaming on the radio
against us
your hoarse sound bytes

(these are your megaphones)

Everyday we see you on the television
posturing your

this is your physical presence
Imperialism is a paper, radio and television tiger
your stripes are a test screen of radiant dots
your fangs are paper macho
your growl a static surge

everyday you ask the lobotomic amnesiac's question

every day you ask the lobotomic amnesiac's question
where does violence come from

let me tell you
it starts with the stealing of the land
the continuing genocide against native people
it comes from the dismemberment of people in other lands
their uprootment and settlement here
in four dollar an hour sweatshops
in the concrete spaceships called
the modern cities
it starts with the kidnapping of native children
it starts with the hudson bay company
and their private police force
(now called the rcmp)
who've ensured the stealing of the furs
who've protected Mr Simpson and Mr Eaton
you ask where violence comes from
from the people who made money off
the african slaves who've worked your farms
the african slaves who've cleaned your homes

ask us where violence comes from
it comes from the great wealth stolen and everyday
it comes from the understanding smile
it comes from your concern about
what all this fuss is about

as if you don't know
and as if you didn't care
as if you hadn't heard

the mail sorters again! damn!
the line didn't work
the word didn't get out!